MW01172059

Dedication

This Self-Care journal is dedication to my 4 beautiful daughters. Thank you for being AMAZING! We have had our ups and downs as a family; however, nothing could ever make you doubt the love I have for you as a mother. I am so honored that GOD chose to use me as the vessel to birth 4 wonderful young ladies. I pray that the life I have lived thus far has encourage and inspired you to seek your own personal relationship with GOD. That even though I love the 4 of you to life! Know that there is no great love then HIS, and as you continue in this journey called life. I pray that each one of you fulfill the purpose GOD has for your life. So, thank you for making me better and know that all the sacrifices were to leave a legacy for you and my grandchildren.

I love you all to life!!!
Mommy

Jeremiah 17:7-8

"Blessed is the man who trusts in the LORD,
And whose hope is the LORD. For he shall be like a tree
planted by the waters,
Which spreads out its roots by the river,
And will not fear when heat comes;
But its leaf will be green,
And will not be anxious in the year of drought,
Nor will cease from yielding fruit.

This scripture lets me know that whatever may come my
way, that if I keep my faith/hope in the LORD. I will
always come out *VICTORIOUS!*

Day 1

"Cry because it hurts, and you need to cleanse yourself!"

Revelation 7:17

_____

_____

_____

_____

_____

_____

_____

_____

_____

_____

_____

_____

_____

_____

_____

_____

_____

_____

_____

Day 2

Get mad! You are human. It is ok to be upset but do not act on it, and do not stay there!

Ephesians 4:26

Day 3

What hurt you?

Matthew 11:28-30

_____
_____
_____
_____
_____
_____
_____
_____
_____
_____
_____
_____
_____
_____
_____
_____
_____
_____
_____
_____
_____
_____
_____
_____
_____
_____

Day 4

Why did this hurt you so bad? Get to the root of the issue
and deal with it.

1 Peter 5:7

_____
_____
_____
_____
_____
_____
_____
_____
_____
_____
_____
_____
_____
_____
_____
_____
_____
_____
_____
_____
_____
_____
_____

Day 5

Forgive, who hurt you!

Colossians 3:13

_____
_____
_____
_____
_____
_____
_____
_____
_____
_____
_____
_____
_____
_____
_____
_____
_____
_____
_____
_____
_____
_____
_____
_____

Day 6

Forgive yourself! Do not beat yourself up, we all have made mistakes in life. Repent, get up, and move forward!

Romans 3:23

_____
_____
_____
_____
_____
_____
_____
_____
_____
_____
_____
_____
_____
_____
_____
_____
_____
_____
_____
_____
_____
_____
_____

Day 7

RELEASE! Yes, I know you are thinking should not that had happened between day 1 and 5. But see the thing is, that you can do all those things and still hold on to it as a crutch.

Galatians 5:1

_____
_____
_____
_____
_____
_____
_____
_____
_____
_____
_____
_____
_____
_____
_____
_____
_____
_____
_____
_____
_____
_____

Day 8

RELAX! Take a day off from everyday life.

Genesis 2:2-3

_____
_____
_____
_____
_____
_____
_____
_____
_____
_____
_____
_____
_____
_____
_____
_____
_____
_____
_____
_____
_____
_____

Day 9

RELAX! A lot has happened and the weight you been carrying was extremely heavy. You need another day of relaxation.

Psalm 62: 1-2

_____
_____
_____
_____
_____
_____
_____
_____
_____
_____
_____
_____
_____
_____
_____
_____
_____
_____
_____
_____
_____
_____
_____

Day 10

RELAX! Yes, I know you're thinking, "I did that for 2 days. I have to get back to work." You do; however, this is the last day. Make it count! Go enjoy a good movie or watch a live band. Whatever but, remember this is the last day of relaxation before you go back to everyday life. So, ENJOY IT!

Psalm 62:5

_____
_____
_____
_____
_____
_____
_____
_____
_____
_____
_____
_____
_____
_____
_____
_____
_____
_____
_____
_____

Day 11

Ok, it's time to get back at it. However, this time let's do
it differently. Let's start our day off with some meditation.

Psalm 49:3

_____
_____
_____
_____
_____
_____
_____
_____
_____
_____
_____
_____
_____
_____
_____
_____
_____
_____
_____
_____
_____
_____
_____
_____
_____

Day 12

Continue to start your day with meditation, but now add affirmation to it.

"I Am Loved by GOD!"

"I Am ANOINTED!"

"I Am BEAUTIFUL/HANDSOME!"

"I Am BLESSED!"

"I Am ENOUGH!"

"I Am FEARFULLLY & WONDERFULLY MADE!"

"I Am RICH!"

"I Am WORTHY!"

These are just some examples, your affirmations maybe different. Whatever they are make sure you AFFIRM YOURSELF daily!

Matthew 6:25-33

_____
_____
_____
_____
_____
_____
_____
_____
_____
_____
_____

Day 13

Start loving yourself! Do your hair! Get a fresh haircut!
Fix yourself up so you can start feeling good about YOU
again!

Song of Solomon 4:7

_____
_____
_____
_____
_____
_____
_____
_____
_____
_____
_____
_____
_____
_____
_____
_____
_____
_____
_____
_____
_____
_____
_____
_____

Day 14

Start taking care of your body! Eat healthy.

1 Corinthians 6:19-20

_____
_____
_____
_____
_____
_____
_____
_____
_____
_____
_____
_____
_____
_____
_____
_____
_____
_____
_____
_____
_____
_____
_____
_____
_____

Day 15

Start exercising at least 3 to 4 times a week. Remember it's about loving YOU!

1 Timothy 4:8

_____
_____
_____
_____
_____
_____
_____
_____
_____
_____
_____
_____
_____
_____
_____
_____
_____
_____
_____
_____
_____
_____
_____
_____

Day 16

Start a new hobby. Whether it's once a week book club or bowling on Tuesday nights. Be selfish and enjoy LIFE!

John 10:10

_____
_____
_____
_____
_____
_____
_____
_____
_____
_____
_____
_____
_____
_____
_____
_____
_____
_____
_____
_____
_____
_____
_____

Day 17

Set a goal or goals that you will accomplish within the next 30 days. However, make sure the goal or goals are aligning with GOD'S purpose for your life.

Proverbs 16:9

_____
_____
_____
_____
_____
_____
_____
_____
_____
_____
_____
_____
_____
_____
_____
_____
_____
_____
_____
_____
_____
_____
_____
_____

Day 18

You are almost there! Only 4 days left, yippee!!! Now,
it's time for your 3 day fast. I know you're thinking
shouldn't I have done this somewhere around day 6. Well,
the purpose for the fast is to hear from GOD doing your
season of planning.

Matthew 6:16-18

_____
_____
_____
_____
_____
_____
_____
_____
_____
_____
_____
_____
_____
_____
_____
_____
_____
_____
_____
_____
_____
_____

Day 19

It's the 2nd day of your fast! Be very careful these 3 days. See the very thing or things you released to GOD; the enemy will try to bring back to hurt you again. So read your word, watch and pray.

Ephesians 6:18

_____
_____
_____
_____
_____
_____
_____
_____
_____
_____
_____
_____
_____
_____
_____
_____
_____
_____
_____
_____
_____
_____

Day 20

This is the last day of your fast and very crucial to your
self-care. Command your day to be AMAZING! Even if it
starts off rocky, know that you have the AUTHORITY to
start your day over at any time. Stay focus on the goal or
goals you set for yourself, read your word, watch, and
pray. Use the wisdom GOD gave, NOT to react to the
distractions the enemy will throw at you.

Philippians 3:13-14

_____

_____

_____

_____

_____

_____

_____

_____

_____

_____

_____

_____

_____

_____

_____

_____

_____

_____

_____

_____

Day 21

You did it!! Today is the last day!! Take yourself out to breakfast. Buy yourself a little something nice. Reflect on all that GOD has DELIVERED, HEALED & SET YOU FREE from! Then celebrate because you have completed your assignment. You took care of YOU!!!

II Timothy 4:7

_____
_____
_____
_____
_____
_____
_____
_____
_____
_____
_____
_____
_____
_____
_____
_____
_____
_____
_____
_____
_____

The purpose for this 21 day of Self-Care was to help you see that at times we can get so engulf with life that we neglect ourselves. And by doing that, that is when depression creeps in along with health issues. We do such a good job taking care of everyone else but ourselves. As if we are not just as important/valuable as the people that are surrounding us. GOD wants you to enjoy life that is why HE gave it to us. In Ecclesiastes 3:12-13 it says, "I know that nothing is better for them than to rejoice, and to do good in their lives, and also that every man should eat and drink and enjoy the good of all his labor – it is the gift of GOD.

Remember to take time out for YOU! You only get ONE life. So, CELEBRATE, ENJOY, EMBRACE & LIVE!!

SELF-CONFIDENCE
is THE BEST OUTFIT
ROCK IT
OWN IT

NOTES

NOTES

NOTES

I pray this journal has help you to HEAL!

Thank you for your love and support!!

Made in the USA
Columbia, SC
17 April 2024

34278171R00024